HENRIETTE MEETS MULLY

MAY RAE

20 Twenty
Literary Group

ISBN
978-1-961250-44-4 (Paperback)
978-1-961250-45-1 (eBook)
978-1-961250-43-7 (Hardcover)

HENRIETTE MEETS MULLY

TABLE OF CONTENTS

INTRODUCTION

Dear Reader,

Thank you for reading our first novel, which numerous conversations, experiences, and places we have shared over the past few years have inspired us. Most notably, Mary acquired the harlequin figurine, which would become Mully, at a Christmas ornament sale at the Maplewood Historical Society's Bruentrup Farm.

An active family member, Marianne Bruentrup, was manning the checkout table. Because Marianne and Rachel both worked in ISD 622 and Mary was a student in the same school district, the women knew each other. Marianne and her mother had cleaned out some boxes of ornaments from years of previous Bruentrup family members' storage.

One piece in particular was a topic of conversation when they bagged and priced the items. The descriptor of "He's so ugly that he's kind of cute" had been attributed to the Mully-to-be through the years. When Marianne saw Mary walk into the barn to check out the tables of sale items, she instinctively knew which item would catch Mary's attention.

**Mary Ayetey, Mully, and Marianne Bruentrup at
Bruentrup Heritage Farm, Maplewood, MN**

After finding a safe place for Mully to sit on the desk in Mary's bedroom, it was only natural that Mully would become a muse and inspire Mary to share her creativity with Rachel. Mary has autism (autism spectrum disorder [ASD]), and she has experienced communication problems, misunderstandings, bullying, and abuse throughout her years of education and transition to adulthood.

There are no easy answers, even if the questions could be asked clearly. For most people with autism, it is nearly impossible to guess what questions need to be asked to dissect and understand any social situation, real or imagined.

Through Mully and Henriette, Mary was able to ask questions she had not been able to express for herself while she was a teenager. As her parent and legal guardian, Rachel was able to think, write, rethink, and rewrite answers through the adults in Henriette's life. This experiment in bibliotherapy became a very important project for mother and daughter.

Although it is a short novel, Henriette and Mully have been living with the McDonald/Ayetey household for several years and are expected to remain cerebral guides toward a better understanding of the past, present, and future. The hope is that you will enjoy this introduction to Henriette as an autistic teenage girl who struggles to make sense of the strange world of neurotypical humans, public education, worldwide web communication, true and false friends, and confidence in herself. The goal is to celebrate life regardless of mislabeled abilities.

Publishing the novel had always been Mary's desire. Although Rachel had not spoken about the project with her brother, Philip, a poem he wrote and posted on Facebook catapulted the story from living room conversation piece to the finished product you are reading. Philip had not met Mully; nor had he visited the Bruentrup Farm. However, his poem spoke very directly to Rachel and Mary. Indeed, what may seem ordinary to us in our neighborhood should be valued as extraordinary.

"We can all strive to do something extraordinary, and in the meantime, we can all enjoy the extraordinary beauty of the ordinary."[1]

Photo of Maplewood Historical Society Bruentrup Heritage Farm by Gary McDonald, August 18, 2018

CHAPTER ONE

"Miss Swanson, what are you reading?" Mr. Graham's inquisitive tone crashed over Henriette like ice water.

Henriette jumped, causing her math book and the novel she was reading to tumble to the floor. The students sitting around her snickered as the books fell.

"*Fifty* what? Is that remedial curriculum?" Mr. Graham directed his question to Marnia, the teaching assistant who always accompanied Henriette to mainstream classrooms.

"Mr. Graham, that book is about sex." A girl pointed an accusatory finger at the public library book on the floor.

"Really?"

"Are you sure?"

"I'll check it out for you!"

A chorus of voices vied to be heard as quickly as the bodies lunged toward the book. The voices swirled around Henriette so quickly that she couldn't tell who was speaking until the last comment. She recognized Juan's voice because she had heard him in the special education resource room working with the reading specialist.

"You can't read," Henriette said, calmly pointing to Juan.

"You can't add. Hell, you can barely count." Juan tossed the book over Henriette's desk.

Henriette swung her arm upward and grabbed the book. She was not aware she had connected with Mr. Graham until she heard him grunt, and the whole classroom erupted in laughter.

"*Fsh*." Mr. Graham's unique hushing sound unfortunately collided with other verbalizations and twisted into Henriette's ear like a worm.

"*Fishuck*," Henriette said.

The classroom became unnaturally quiet for one millisecond and then laughter, hushing sounds, and groans ricocheted off the walls, attacking Henriette's ears.

"*Fishuck*! *Fishuck*!" Henriette yelled louder and banged her head on the top of her desk.

"That's enough," Mr. Graham said. "Henriette, go with, umm, your aide …"

"Her name is Marnia. You keep forgetting that." Juan, the boy who had thrown the book, shot a concerned look at Henriette.

"Thank you, Juan. No, Lou, you stay in your seat," Mr. Graham said.

"I'm Luke, Mr. Graham. I know remembering everyone's name is difficult for a substitute teacher the first few weeks. I'm happy to help Henriette. I understand her," Luke said smoothly and smiled innocently at the substitute teacher.

"She's not going to be in one of your brother's porno videos," whispered Juan.

"It's called art, cowboy." Luke smirked but didn't sit down until Marnia placed herself between Henriette and him.

"It's okay," Marnia said. "I've got this."

Mr. Graham nodded curtly and then commanded, "Math, people. Today we are talking about multiplying and dividing fractions. Take out a sheet of paper for a three-minute comprehension drill."

Through the cacophony of groans, jeers, and Mr. Graham's voice ordering everyone's attention back to their textbooks, Marnia's soft voice directed Henriette. "It's okay, Henriette. Follow the standard operating procedure: book in backpack. Backpack on shoulder. Look at my shoulder. Hold my arm. Follow me."

"I'm sorry," Henriette said.

She didn't know what had happened, but she always felt like everything was her fault. Usually people's voices got quieter when she said "I'm sorry." The quietness helped her control her arms so they didn't swing out and hit anyone.

Marnia closed the door behind them when they got into the hallway, but Henriette could still hear Mr. Graham's voice.

"Oh no!" Henriette moaned. "I'm in trouble again."

Out in the hallway, Marnia held up a card with a picture of a cloud blowing a puff of wind. Marnia held up three fingers. Henriette took three deep breaths. Next, Marnia fanned out a handful of cards and held them toward Henriette. Henriette picked an overhead-arm stretch picture, and both Marnia and Henriette did the stretch in continued silence.

Mr. Graham stepped out of his classroom, right into the hallway.

"I'm sorry," Henriette said.

"I know." Mr. Graham nodded.

"Am I in trouble?" Henriette asked.

"It's not conversation time yet," Marnia said as she directed Henriette's attention back to the cards. She held up the deep breath card and modeled a slow, deep breath.

Both Henriette and Mr. Graham followed her.

"Now it is conversation time," Marnia said.

"I'm sorry," Henriette said again.

"I understand you're sorry." Mr. Graham nodded. "But I don't know what we can do differently."

"What do we need to do next, Mr. Graham?" Marnia asked.

"You will need to take her to the principal's office. We need to follow procedure and call in the school counselor because she did hit me and she is reading a book during math class for the second time since I took over the class."

"It's fourth actually. You didn't notice the other two times," Henriette said while she sat on the floor, holding her head in her hands.

"Thank you for being honest, Henriette. Nevertheless, your choice of reading material is not appropriate for any classroom in this school. Not even sex education, so we are going to have to let Vice Principal King make the decision of what to do next."

"C'mon, Henriette. I'll walk with you," said Marnia. "I talk to VP King all the time. It's no big deal." Marnia offered her hand to help Henriette stand up.

Henriette shook her head. "I can do it myself." She stood up and lightly held Marnia's elbow as they walked to the office.

Chapter Two

Henriette's mother and stepfather, Bernice and George Appleton, walked into the principal's office together.

"What happened now?" Bernice asked sternly.

"I was reading a book," Henriette answered.

"Why would a student be in trouble for reading a book?" George looked around the office accusingly.

Vice Principal King ushered the family into her office and handed George the pornographic novel Henriette had been reading. "Because she was reading this book from the public library during math class."

George adjusted his bifocals and then laughed aloud, "Hey, Neecie, maybe. Oof!" George stopped talking when Bernice jabbed him in the side with her elbow.

"George, this is neither the time nor the place." Bernice took the book out of George's hands and stuffed it into her handbag. "I will make sure this gets returned immediately. And I will hold on to your library card, Miss Rita, until we can decide how to better monitor your choices."

"Mom, don't call me Rita. I'm not a kid anymore."

Before either Bernice or George could respond, VP King intervened. "I understand you are recently married, in the middle of a remodeling project, and planning a trip as well? I am sure there are lots of new challenges. Extra things to get organized."

"We are behind schedule," George said.

"I liked the house better before George moved in. It wasn't so messy," Henriette said.

"Remodeling is always messy. It has to get worse before it gets better," Bernice replied.

"That doesn't make sense," Henriette answered.

VP King intervened again. "Have you been able to take advantage of any respite opportunities?"

"Send her with strangers?" Bernice asked.

"What respite opportunities?" George inquired.

"I want to quit school. I have the right to quit school when I am sixteen. I can stay in my bedroom. I like my bedroom." Henriette started picking anxiously at a loose string hanging from the hem of her shirt.

George laughed.

This made Henriette get angrier. "Screw you, brasshole. I quit! So there!"

"Stop with the fake swear words, Henriette," ordered Bernice. "Dropping out of school is not an option."

Bernice took an MP3 player and headphones out of her handbag and handed them to Henriette, who put them on immediately.

"Our counselor is not available to meet with you today, but she did ask me to pass on the information she has about respite services. In some cases, we are able to write an addendum to the IEP, allowing for remote classroom learning for a couple of weeks throughout the school year, if you choose a respite provider outside of the school district. We are not recommending any specific respite provider. We just want to make sure you are aware of all your options."

"My sister used to host international students at her farm," George stated. "She has invited Henriette to stay with her in a couple weeks during spring break. Would she qualify?"

"You would need to check with your social worker to verify eligibility, but as long as there is an internet connection for logging into the cyber classroom option and Henriette keeps up with assignments online, it would meet our requirements on a short-term basis. Improving social interaction with peers is an IEP goal that needs to be addressed, of course. However, the biggest concern right now is resolving her choices in math class and how it impacts her future decision regarding completing her education." VP King looked pointedly at Bernice as she emphasized the word *her* each time she said it.

"This is the second long-term substitute teacher for math class. The inconsistency in teachers is not *her* problem," Bernice spat through clenched teeth.

George squeezed her wrist, and Bernice pursed her lips.

"Henriette," George said, "I want to be sure you understand your options. One option is to stay at home with a tutor to complete assignments while the construction workers are doing the remodeling. The second option is to stay with my sister and her husband, your Aunt Lisa and Uncle Blake, at their farm. It is only for two weeks. Do you understand the options?"

"Yes, but what if I want to drop out?"

"Dropping out is not an option this year." VP King stressed the word *this* and shot a silencing glance toward Bernice. "You have option one to stay at the house with somebody approved by the school. Or you have option two, which is staying with your Aunt Lisa and Uncle Blake at their farm."

"The construction in the house is going to be noisy and dirty. Some people think farms are noisy and dirty, but your Aunt Lisa runs a tight ship," George said.

"She has a ship on the farm?" Henriette asked.

"I'm sorry. I keep forgetting that the idioms I use don't always make sense to you. She does not have a ship, but she likes everything to be clean and organized. Uncle Blake even must keep his woodshop and motorcycle workshop neat and tidy. Some people call that shipshape, but it's just a funny way of saying structured and predictable."

"Can I ride a motorcycle?" Henriette asked.

"Yes," answered George.

"No," replied Bernice at the exact same moment.

"I like structure. I think I will try staying at the farm. But if I don't like it, I will let you know. Is that a deal, George?" Henriette asked.

"Yes, my girl, that is a deal. Let's shake on it." George put his hand out to shake hands with Henriette, and then they both did a hand jive dance and ended with a high five.

"Okay, I guess that's settled for now," Bernice said, unable to keep from smiling at George and Henriette. "We will need to get the textbooks."

"I was thinking of ordering books on Amazon," Henriette said. "I would like to order mythology, history, French, Spanish, German, Arabic, and science."

"Henriette, it's only two weeks!" Bernice exclaimed.

"Neecie, she's motivated, and that's great. Henriette, I will send Lisa an email and tell her what you want to learn. She knows how to read IEPs, and she's got shelves of books. I am confident she can help you find something that interests you. If she doesn't have a book you want, I will order it and have it delivered to the farm," George said as he stood up. "If that's settled, I'd like to take my ladies out for supper."

Bernice glared at VP King and then back at George. "You know this only delays—"

"I know," George said as he opened the door. "This is a good option for now."

CHAPTER THREE

On the day Henriette moved to her aunt's farm, she felt nervous about the change. Excitement replaced her nervousness when she saw the neat red barns and large white farmhouse with green shutters. One small building near the house was an activity room for crafts, music classes, exercising, and dancing. The barns farther away from the house had animals, which Henriette was looking forward to meeting. She found it easier to talk to animals than people.

Henriette was quiet as Aunt Lisa showed her the guest bedroom she would be staying in.

"I am sure you will want to ask me some questions later, but right now is a good time to get comfortable in your room. I will be back in ten minutes to give you a tour of the rest of the house. Then we will have lunch. After lunch, we can work on our schedule for the rest of the day. Does that sound like a good plan?"

"Okay," Henriette said.

Aunt Lisa started to speak again but changed her mind when she observed Henriette standing awkwardly in the middle of the room, staring at the floor. Aunt Lisa took a deep breath and quietly closed the door.

Henriette stared into space and let the picture of her bedroom at the farmhouse move into her vision, like snapshots floating across a screen. She liked her bedroom because it was painted dark orange and had a wallpaper border with pictures of wolves. The wolves looked quietly proud and confident. She especially liked the picture of the mother wolf and pups.

Henriette sat down on the floor and leaned her back against her bed, tilting her head back so she could look at the border pictures. Out loud, she said, "The pups' names are Nova and Bonami."

A voice from the bookshelf said, "Those are nice names. I always call the littlest pup Binky, but in real life, an adult wolf would not want to have a baby name like Binky."

Henriette froze in place and asked, "Who's there?"

"I'm not there. I am here. And my name is Mully."

"Where?" asked Henriette.

"Look at the bookshelf," said Mully. "I am in the middle of the top shelf."

Henriette walked over to the bookshelf and searched the middle shelf. "Where?" she inquired once more.

"Look up at the top shelf. Now point your finger toward the middle."

"Oh, I see you. What are you?"

"I am a farm fairy today. I come from all around the world and have different names in different countries and different states. I find people who are sad, and I make them happy. Do you remember my name?"

"No."

"Mully. My name is Mully."

"Hi, Mully. My name is Henriette. I am pleased to meet you."

"Thank you, Henriette. I am pleased to meet you too. You have very good manners."

"I know," said Henriette. "I can say some things, but I don't like to talk that much."

"Why not?"

"I have autism. That means I don't understand people very well, and most people don't understand me. I get annoyed when they keep saying 'I don't know what you mean.' People say that to me a lot, and they call me names like retard and crazy girl."

"How does that make you feel?"

"Mad. I want to tell all of them to shut the fuck up. But then I get in trouble for not using manners. It's confusing."

"What do you do when you're confused?" Mully asked.

"I want to punch them, but I know I shouldn't. So I think it's better if I hurt myself."

"I understand," said Mully. "It will make me sad if I see you hurt yourself."

"I know," replied Henriette. "I'm tired now. I don't want to talk anymore."

"I can respect that," answered Mully. "I will be here when you want to visit me."

CHAPTER FOUR

On the first day of homeschool with Aunt Lisa, Henriette was very quiet. She did not say one word the whole morning.

"Henriette, may I ask you a personal question?"

Henriette looked up at Aunt Lisa for a brief second. "Sure."

"Why were you reading that pornographic book?"

"For writing class."

"Do you have the assignment sheet? Or is it online?"

"Yes, I have it." Henriette pulled out a folded, dirty sheet of paper.

Aunt Lisa unfolded the sheet and put on her reading glasses. "That's interesting. It looks like the assignment is for a compare-and-contrast paper. Two to four paragraphs. It says here you could read two articles. Why did you choose two books?"

Henriette froze. "I … ah … I dunno."

Aunt Lisa took off her reading glasses and spoke reassuringly. "I'm sure you had a good reason."

"I can't remember," Henriette mumbled.

"It's okay. Take a deep breath. You can be honest with me. I will respect your privacy. Where were you when you made this choice?"

"In the Maplewood library. At my favorite table in the back."

"Good, so there you were at your favorite table in the library. You had *Beauty and the Beast*, and you were starting your assignment. Then what picture came into your mind?"

"I made this list: Belle is scared but brave and curious. She gets locked in a room. She has to learn to trust Beast to earn her freedom."

Aunt Lisa said, "That's a good start. So then you needed to compare it to another story. How did you make that decision?"

Henriette shrugged. "I saw the previews for the movie. I saw some girls reading it on the bus, and I didn't want everyone to think I only read little kid stories. Plus, it was kind of just sitting there."

"In the library?" Aunt Lisa asked.

"Yeah, some kids were reading it, and then Luke tossed it in the chair next to me and left."

"Hmm, how fortuitous."

"What?" asked Henriette.

"Nothing, dear. Let's try to get this done quickly. In a compare-and-contrast paper, it's good to find at least two things that are the same and two that are different. What two things were the same?"

"I wrote it here. Both Belle and Anastasia were held prisoner and had to earn their freedom by learning to trust."

Aunt Lisa looked out the window and took a deep breath. Then she slowly asked, "And how were they different?"

Henriette gave Aunt Lisa a quizzical look. "One was a beast, and one was a man, of course."

Aunt Lisa stacked the books to one side. "Okay, I think that's enough about communication. Let's get started on something else."

Henriette said, "You're frustrated with me."

Aunt Lisa looked shocked, and tears welled up in her eyes. "No, no, I'm not frustrated with you at all. I think you … Well, I think you are very creative and your reading skills are excellent. I am only going to be your teacher for two weeks. My decision is to give you an A for your oral report of the compare-and-contrast assignment. I think I can be much more helpful to you in math."

"Math sucks. I want to quit school. I have the right to quit school when I am sixteen."

"I understand you don't like the math you have to learn at your school. But here at Aunt Lisa's homeschool, math is fun. The first thing we are going to do is sort these beads. Then we will count and record the number for each color. We will calculate percent, and then the really fun part happens. We will use the beads to make earrings."

Later, Henriette could hear Aunt Lisa on the phone. She got anxious because Aunt Lisa sounded angry.

"You should have warned me. No, not Bernice. You, George. That is my point exactly. You do not know anything! All right, to be fair, you do not know as much as I would like you to know. You need to take some responsibility in this. All you told me was there was a misunderstanding on her IEP. Let me tell you what I have observed just this morning: ASD presenting with Lexile measure over twelve hundred, scattered comprehension, poor social navigation skills, and dyscalculia, all of which are leading to depression. In my opinion, this is not a little misunderstanding. George, I am your big sister. I love you to bits, and I am over-the-moon happy you have finally fallen in love with a truly wonderful woman.

"Let me finish. Of course I can handle this. Henriette is a dream compared to some I've worked with. I am postponing my full lecture for you, George, but you will hear what I have to say when you return. I love you too. Give Bernice a hug and kiss from me. You two relax and enjoy yourselves."

CHAPTER FIVE

Henriette woke up while it was still dark outside. She was thinking about the words she had heard Aunt Lisa say to George. It made her feel uncomfortable, and she thought, *Maybe I did something wrong.*

She went down to the kitchen table and found the box of beads. She took out the tools and made a pair of earrings the way she had learned when her neighbor's Girl Scout team taught a class. Then she got herself a snack and went back up to her room.

"Mully, are you awake?" Henriette asked.

"Yes, I'm right here," Mully answered. "What are you thinking about?"

"I don't know if I will like being outside at the farm. I'm afraid of getting stung by a bee or a mosquito."

Mully said, "I feel comfortable outside. The bees and mosquitoes fly wherever they need to. They don't follow marked roads like humans do. Sometimes humans get in the way and think the bugs are after them, but really the insect's brain is too small to think like that. They are just following their sense of smell or touch to find something they need. You can wear insect repellent that makes you smell disgusting to them so they won't want to land on you. However, if you walk in front of them, they will buzz in your ear. That's a good thing though. It's just like a car honking its horn to say, 'Watch out! Passing through!'

"Being out in the countryside can be very calming once you are prepared for some of the surprises. You can carry a fan, and you can use bug spray. If the insects don't bother you, then there's no reason to interfere. Whatever you do, don't try one time, give up, and spend the rest of your life inside, closed off from the outdoor world. You will miss out on some of the most beautiful magical discoveries. What is something you find outside that makes you feel comfortable?"

"Trees. The sun. Flowers." Henriette yawned. "Thanks, Mully. Good night."

CHAPTER SIX

"I have looked through the suggested lesson plans and your IEP goals. It seems to me you are ahead of schedule in everything except math," said Aunt Lisa on the second day of Henriette's visit.

"Math sucks," said Henriette. "Are you mad at George?"

"Why do you think I'm mad at George?"

"You said he should have warned you. Did you mean about me because I hate math?"

Aunt Lisa reached for an empty shoebox and her container of empty thread spools. "Let me restate what I am hearing in our conversation, okay?"

"Okay," replied Henriette.

"I have heard four different conversation starters." Aunt Lisa took four spools and put them in the box. "I also am thinking about one thing that I would really like to discuss with you. Altogether, how many different conversations could we have if each of these spools equals one idea?" Aunt Lisa pointed to the box.

"One, two, three, four, five," Henriette replied, counting out loud.

Aunt Lisa took a spool out of the box and placed it on the table in front of Henriette as she explained each topic. "We could talk about brother-and-sister relationships. We could talk about the social rules regarding listening to other people's conversations, IEP goals, or lesson plans. Or we could talk about math. What would you like to talk about first?"

Henriette picked up the first spool and handed it to Aunt Lisa. "Brothers and sisters."

"Every family is a little bit different even though many things are the same. Families need to share, work together, and respect each other. How a brother and sister talk to each other will be a little bit different in every family. I am only going to explain what is the same and what is different between George and me. I am older than he is. I like to be in quiet places. I like to read a lot of books to learn new things.

"George is younger than I am. When he was a teenager, he enjoyed being in noisy, crowded places where there was lots of music, dancing, talking, and laughing. When he was home alone, he would turn on the radio and the TV at the same time. He also loved to read, but he mostly liked to learn about new things by doing them. He never worried about how many mistakes he made. I tried to help him when I thought he was making too many mistakes. Sometimes he liked my help, and other times he didn't. As adults, George and I may argue and sound angry, but we always love and respect each other. Does that make sense?"

"Yes, that's very nice. I don't have a brother or a sister."

"I know. What would you like to talk about next?"

"I don't want to talk about math. You choose."

"Eavesdropping is the word we use for listening to other people's conversations. However, I will take responsibility for this one because I should have gone to a private place to have a discreet conversation. With all the cell phones these days, I'm not even sure what the social rule about eavesdropping is anymore. Do you?"

"Not really. What is a lesson plan?"

"How do you think teachers decide what to talk about each day?"

"I don't know. Maybe the principal tells them."

"A team of people decides what needs to be taught each day in a public school. That is called the curriculum. Each teacher decides how he is going to teach the curriculum by making his own schedule. Do you use schedules at home?"

"Yes, the morning schedule before school and the bedtime schedule at night. I have schedules at school too. Sometimes I make my own. Other times a teacher gives me a schedule."

"A teacher makes a schedule for teaching a subject, and that schedule is a lesson plan. In my homeschool, if I were going to teach a class on counting by fives, I would write a lesson plan like this. First, I would have the students count to five on their fingers. Then I would give each one a handful of pennies and have all of them make stacks of five. Then I would have them trade their five pennies for a nickel and two nickels for a dime. Then when it is time for the lesson, I would bring my sheet of paper with me, that is, my lesson plan. And I would bring the supplies I need. I would know what coins to bring because I wrote it down on my lesson plan. Does that make sense?"

"Yes."

"We are down to the last two conversation starters, IEP and math. Luckily they go together. Do you know what IEP means?"

"Individual education program or something. We have IEP meetings because I have autism."

"Individualized educational plan. You should get to choose some of the things on your IEP, but the law requires some of the things, like math."

"I hate—"

"Uh-uh. I'm sorry for interrupting, but the first thing I want to do is make a pact. You and I will not say 'I hate math' during the days that you get to be with me. Is that a deal?"

"Yes," Henriette replied robotlike, automatically.

"Second, I am going to introduce you to a special math book I have from Shanghai, China, that teaches most of the same math you have seen before at your school. There's something special about it that I think you will like. This math book uses some French words for an easy kind of measuring. The International System of Units is called SI because it's abbreviated from the French words *Le Système International d'Unités*, but we know it as metric. Metric is much easier to say than *Le Système International d'Unités*, isn't it?" Aunt Lisa smiled reassuringly at Henriette.

"I want to learn French and other languages too," said Henriette.

"That's great. Guess what? You already know some of the French words."

"I do?"

"Yes, you know the words *liter* and *meter*."

"And gram," Henriette said. "Mr. Graham told us how much he weighed in grams. It was a big number, I think. I don't remember. Will Mr. Graham be angry if I use a different book?"

"I do not believe he should be. I want you to give it a try. Tell me which parts of the book you like and which parts you don't. At the end of our two weeks together, I will write a letter to your math teacher and tell him what we did.

"Now let's take a break and go collect some eggs so I can make omelets for lunch. We can set the timer for one hour. That's when we'll start our first math class."

Chapter Seven

After Henriette finished eating her lunch and washing her dishes, Aunt Lisa told her, "Let's make a schedule first. When you are doing something difficult, how much breaktime do you think you will need?

"Ten minutes", she said.

"It will be easier for me to schedule two five-minute breaks. Is that okay with you?"

"Yes."

"What do you like to do for your breaks?"

"Listen to music, play Reverie harp, write songs, or color in butterfly or classic cars coloring books."

"Good. Here's the schedule. We will start with listening to one song, which will be your choice. Next, we will work on adding and subtracting measurements, but we won't use any fractions. Do you know what this is?" Aunt Lisa held up a meter stick.

"A yardstick?" Henriette guessed.

"It's a little shorter than a yardstick. This is a meter stick. The nice thing about metric is there is no reason to convert fourths to eighths, multiply by two, and then divide by whatever just to build a flower box with Uncle Blake in the woodshop."

"I thought I had to work on math."

"Woodshop uses a lot of math. It's simpler in metric because we don't have to deal with fractions. After we start building the box, we will work on a couple of math pages. Then you can take another break. What would you like to choose for your second break?"

"Play harp and djembe."

"Good. After harp and djembe, we will work on another type of math-related job called quality control, or QC. Do you know what that means?"

"No, I don't think so."

"It's not something you may hear a lot about, but it is a very important job that is a part of almost everything that we use each day. I'll start with a simple example. Do you see these three bags of candies? We are going to pretend that we work for a very strict boss who wants exactly ten of each color of candy. We sort, count, record, and compare the three bags. Then we will create a perfect bag for our boss, and if we're lucky, we will have some leftovers to add to the cookies we are going to make tomorrow. How does the schedule look to you?"

"Good, I guess. My brain is getting full now."

"Let's get started. First, we will put on our work boots and go to the woodshop. Once we get there, Uncle Blake will talk about tools and safety. He will show you the pattern for a flower box and the building supplies. Ready?"

Henriette got up and walked toward her bedroom.

Aunt Lisa sat still in her chair, her eyebrows raised slightly. "Henriette, did you forget something?"

"No."

"Actually you did. It's a social rule that you answer if a teacher asks you a question like 'Are you ready?'"

"I'm getting ready. My boots are in my room."

"I know, but it is a social rule to make eye contact and answer with your words before you walk away."

Henriette clenched her fists, sucked in her cheeks, and bit down hard on the soft skin until the pain made her eyes water.

Aunt Lisa broke eye contact and spoke softly. "I'm sorry if I said something that upset you."

From the upstairs room, Henriette could hear Mully singing. "Breathe. Just breathe. Breathe and trust."

Henriette took one slow breath and asked, "Can I have an honest word with you?"

"Yes, of course," said Aunt Lisa

"I don't like to work on social rules and math at the same time. My brain gets too full."

"Fair enough. I will meet you outside when you are ready."

Uncle Blake's workshop had one very clean area where there was a table and a chalkboard. Most of the rest of the workshop was a beautiful mess of hand tools on the wall, machines, piles of wood, sawdust, and two large shelves of projects in varying stages of production.

CHAPTER EIGHT

Uncle Blake's large frame filled the workshop. His loud voice was cheerful as he greeted Henriette. "Hi, Henriette. Welcome to my workshop. I call this math lesson 'Making a Flower Box with Uncle Blake.' Are you ready?"

"I guess." Henriette nodded.

"Great! Safety in the woodshop is very important. Lots of fun stuff are in here for making lots of cool things, but there are also lots of ways to get hurt if you are not paying attention. Safety rule number one is listening to me. If I say stop, you need to stop immediately. Then ask yourself, 'Why?'

"With the younger students, I play a game like red light/green light, where I give an instruction like 'Pick up the hammer.' Then I say 'Stop!' until they can stop without touching the hammer before I let them start using it. Do you want to play the game?"

"Okay," Henriette said tensely.

Uncle Blake put a hammer and a hatchet on the table in front of Henriette. "Each one is labeled. Pick up the hatchet. Stop."

Henriette wrapped her hand around the handle of the hatchet and then felt Uncle Blake staring at her. She stopped, unsure of what to do next. She felt like she had done something wrong, but she wasn't sure.

She glanced up at Uncle Blake's face. "Oh, I wasn't paying attention," she stated, guessing from the half-smile, half-scowl expression on his face.

"That's okay," said Uncle Blake. "It takes a few tries to get it right. Remember, I'm going to tell you to pick up a tool. Be ready for a change though. If I say 'Stop!' you have to stop immediately." He continued, "Let's try again. Pick up the hammer. Stop."

Henriette stopped with her hand just above the hammer.

"Good. One more time. Pick up the hammer." This time he did not tell Henriette to stop.

Henriette paused and then picked it up. "Now what?"

"I'll help you figure out where to put it away. In my woodshop, there is a place for everything, and everything needs to be returned to its place. Look toward the wall. Do you see anything on the wall that looks like the hammer in your hand?"

"There's a big hammer hanging on the wall over there."

"Right. Start walking in that direction. Let me know when you see an empty space that looks the right size for your hammer."

"Can I have a hammer of my own?" Henriette asked.

"You bet," Uncle Blake answered.

"No, I don't," Henriette mumbled, confused.

Henriette walked toward the wall where the hammers were hanging. Uncle Blake walked behind her, steadying the items Henriette bumped into in the unfamiliar workroom.

"No worries. People always bump into things the first time through the workshop." Uncle Blake started whistling a slightly off-pitch variation of the *Sesame Street* theme song, "Sunny Day."

Henriette stopped suddenly. "Is that where it goes?" She pointed to the empty outline of a hammer on the wall in front of her.

"You bet," Uncle Blake answered enthusiastically and patted Henriette's shoulder.

"No, I don't," Henriette said vehemently and spun around to face Uncle Blake.

"Are you talking to the ghosts?" Uncle Blake asked.

"I don't like people touching me and talking behind my back!" Henriette shouted. "I'm not a retard, and I'm not a criminal." Angrily she threw the hammer at Uncle Blake.

"What the fuck?" Uncle Blake exclaimed as the hammer hit his upper lip.

In her mind, Henriette was thinking, *That is a bad word. Teachers are not supposed to say the F-word in front of students.* With her anxiety increasing, autism-driven echolalia took over, and the only word she could make her head think was *fuck*.

"Fuck, fuck," Henriette said uncontrollably. She hit her head against the workbench to get the sound loop in her head to stop.

Aunt Lisa was feeling very peaceful as she walked into the workshop with several eggs in her hands. Then she saw Blake's bleeding lip and Henriette banging her head on the workbench, and she dropped the eggs, breaking them all, and ran the last few steps.

"Wha—" She snapped her head back and forth from Blake to Henriette as if she were watching a very fast ping-pong match.

Blake looked confused and put his hands up hopelessly. "I don't know what happened to her," he said, bewildered.

"I can help," Aunt Lisa said, bending near Henriette. "Walk with me to the house."

"Mu-u-ll-y-y!" Henriette yelled, finally getting a picture in her head of her friend, which helped interrupt the echolalia.

Henriette jumped up and ran straight through the workshop, avoiding the stacks of unfinished wood and the broken eggs on the floor. She ran into the house and up the stairs to her room. She grabbed Mully off the shelf and plopped herself down on her bed.

"I know," Mully said inside her head. "You don't have to use any words with me. I know how to think in pictures."

CHAPTER NINE

"What happened?" Aunt Lisa asked Blake.

"Like I said, I don't know," Blake answered. "Let's see. I guess I can walk you through it. We started over here with the safety lesson. Then we walked over here. She said something, and I asked her if she were talking to ghosts. Then she yelled something about not being a criminal or a retard. She threw the hammer and ran. I don't think she wanted to hurt me. I've got the Harley on blocks over here, and she ran around it. She looked like a wild animal wanting to escape."

Lisa retraced Blake and Henriette's steps. "When you finished the safety game, who walked in front?"

"She did."

"Show me," Lisa commanded.

"What do you mean? I just walked like this." Blake walked and whistled.

"You were whistling the *Sesame Street* theme?" Lisa asked accusingly.

"I don't know. It's just a tune I whistle. You think my whistling set her off?" Blake looked like he was close to tears.

"It can be irritating." Lisa softened the criticism with a smile. "Why did you ask her about ghosts?"

"She yelled 'No, I don't!' out of the blue. Then she yelled something about criminal and retard, threw the hammer, and ran. I saw mostly fear though, not anger." Blake looked back to where Henriette was standing when she started yelling. He furrowed his brow in concentration, trying to puzzle through the string of events.

"I understand part of it, but it seems like something is missing. I'm sorry about your lip." Lisa tried to tend to Blake's injury, but he shooed her away.

"You don't need to babysit me. You know I've looked worse. Go check on the kid and let me know when it's safe to come inside."

Lisa stopped to clean up the broken eggs, but Blake took the broom and dustpan away from her. "I'll clean this up. Go."

In the house, Lisa could hear Henriette talking to herself in her bedroom. As Lisa walked up the stairs, she could clearly hear what Henriette was saying. She didn't know Henriette had her headphones on, listening to music, but also talking to Mully.

"I was walking toward the hammer wall like he said, and he was whistling the little kid's songs. Then he started talking behind my back so I couldn't practice the eye contact because I have to do that. Everyone tells me, but I hate it. And Marnia said I don't like people talking about me behind my back, and I got confused." Henriette's voice droned in nonstop monotone.

As she took a breath, she heard Mully's voice. "Were you scared?"

"I'm not scared of Uncle Blake. He's nice so I don't know why he was talking behind my back and said 'You bet.' I can't go to a casino until I am older. I don't gamble. I don't like pornography. I'm not a criminal. I can't multitask. I can't do social rules and work at the same time. My brain got so blind that I couldn't see any pictures. Then he said the word he isn't supposed to say, and my brain was all fuzzy, like water going too fast, crashing on a pizza pan in the sink. Bang! Bang! Bang!"

"You are a good person," Mully said. "Take a deep breath. I will try to help you talk to Aunt Lisa and Uncle Blake."

"I can't talk," Henriette said. "I don't know how words work with humans. I can't ... I can't ... I can't talk the right words."

"Can you sing?" asked Mully. "I like this song."

Henriette and Mully sang together, "I see a bad moon a-rising. I see trouble on its way."

Aunt Lisa stood at Henriette's door. She could not hear Mully's voice, of course, so she thought Henriette was talking to herself. As Aunt Lisa listened to Henriette's monologue, she imagined what Henriette heard and saw. She finally understood the confusion and silently laughed.

She put her hand over her mouth to stifle the sound and ran down the stairs. She dropped into a chair at the kitchen table and laughed out loud as she pictured her dear, bumbling husband and precious Henriette trying to communicate. She laughed until tears rolled down her face.

Blessed with exceptionally good hearing, Henriette could hear noises from downstairs, even though she and Mully were singing.

"Wait. Stop," Henriette said. "What was that?"

She walked downstairs and found Aunt Lisa in the kitchen. "Are you crying?"

"No. Well, yes. Do you know what tears of laughter are?"

"No," said Henriette tentatively.

"Sometimes people laugh so hard that their eyes water," Aunt Lisa tried to explain.

"Were you laughing at me?" Henriette asked, starting to build her imaginary angry wall.

"No, dear, no. I was laughing at myself and at Uncle Blake. We made some big mistakes, and I hope you will forgive us."

"I hurt Uncle Blake. That was a mistake," Henriette said while staring at Aunt Lisa's shoulder. It was the closest thing to eye contact that she could manage.

"Yes, that mistake was not funny. Uncle Blake will forgive you because you were confused. You did not mean to hurt him. The funny mistake I was laughing about was how we got our words mixed up."

Henriette looked confused.

Aunt Lisa wiped the moisture from her eyes and took a deep, centering breath. "I'd like to explain something to you. Do you have room in your brain for some new information?"

"Is it about math?" Henriette asked.

"No, it's about words," Aunt Lisa reassured her. "And there's a funny cheer I want to teach you."

"Okay," Henriette answered.

"Great! You just said okay, and that gave me a picture in my brain that you are calm and ready to get some new information from me."

Aunt Lisa showed Henriette the drawing she had started. There were two people each with a thinking bubble and a talking circle drawn next to them. "Here is your work, and here is my thinking bubble with a picture of you sitting calmly with your head open to get new information. Our heads don't really open up like that, do they? We get our information through our ears, eyes, and noses. Does that make sense?"

"Yes."

"Good," Aunt Lisa continued. "That's a lot of information for me to get when all you said was one two-letter word. But it was enough. You didn't have to say the whole sentence like a robot, 'Yes, I am calm and able to listen to your words.'"

Henriette laughed "I'm not a robot."

"No, of course not." Aunt Lisa smiled. "Some people grew up saying two words, which means the same thing as *okay* means to you and me. Are you ready for this?"

"Okay." Henriette nodded her head.

"They say, 'You bet!' It doesn't mean anything about gambling at a casino. It's shortened for 'Ya sure you betcha.' Can I teach you a funny cheer from Uncle Blake's high school?"

Henriette nodded.

"It goes like this." Aunt Lisa cleared her throat. "Lutefisk, lutefisk, leftsa, leftsa. We're da mighty Vikings. Ya mon, you betcha."

Aunt Lisa and Henriette laughed together.

"What does that mean?" Henriette asked.

Lisa laughed. "It's a funny cheer Uncle Blake learned from his friends, who learned it from their cousins. I don't know where it started, but it makes me laugh every time I hear it. The important thing I am trying to tell you is that Uncle Blake says 'You bet!' when he means 'okay.' I call it Blake-talk. He has his own way of saying things sometimes. I would like you to practice speaking Blake-talk with me. Give me a high five."

Henriette held up her hand for a high five.

"Great!" Aunt Lisa smiled. "Let's do high fives again, but this time when our hands touch, we will shout, 'You bet!' Ready? One, two, three."

"You bet!" the two chorused as they slapped their hands together.

"Does it make sense to you that Uncle Blake was saying 'ok' when he said 'you bet'?"

"Yes, but he still shouldn't talk behind my back," Henriette said seriously.

"Ah, the problem with idioms again. Let's keep this simple. Yes, you are right. Uncle Blake needs to make sure he is looking at you when he speaks to you so you can feel comfortable. Does that sound like a good rule for us to give Uncle Blake?"

"Yes," Henriette answered. "My brain is full now. Can I take a break?"

"Yes, of course. We can meet back here at the kitchen table in thirty minutes. I will explain a few things to Blake first, and then the two of you can have a talk here at the kitchen table."

Exactly thirty minutes later, Henriette paced restlessly at the bottom of the steps. She did not look directly at Uncle Blake, but she could see him motion with his hand for her to come across the table from him. He placed a glass of ice water and a plate of crackers in front of her. Henriette was relieved his eyes were staring at the plate of crackers between them instead of staring into her eyes. She didn't know why other people could handle the pain of eye contact better than she could. It was a big relief to her that Uncle Blake wasn't staring at her when he spoke to her this time.

"Let me see if I understand what happened," Uncle Blake said. "First, the song I was whistling sounded like something from preschool, so you thought I was treating you like a child. Then because I said "You bet!" you thought I was accusing you of gambling and being a criminal. So that made you angry. That's a big surprise to me, but you know what? It makes sense now that you and Lisa have explained it to me.

"I also understand having difficulty with social rules. I have some trouble with that myself. Or at least I did until your Aunt Lisa helped me get a few things figured out, especially when talking to police officers. I'm curious though. How do you know about criminals and gambling? Has anyone else talked to you about doing something illegal?"

"Yeah, but I'm not supposed to talk about it with adults."

"That's okay," said Uncle Blake. "I'll let you in on a little secret. I have been accused of being a lot of things, but I have never been told I'm acting too much like an adult. Who told you not to talk about illegal stuff with adults?"

"Luke said it's not illegal, but adults don't understand because they don't know about internet laws."

"I see. What does Luke say to you when he talks to you?"

"You can trust me. I want to be your friend. Would you like to be in my brother's video? Stuff like that. And sometimes he explains the math to me and helps me get answers on the worksheets. So that's nice."

"What is the video about?"

"Music, swimsuits, and reading."

"Reading?" Blake inquired. Then he started to get it. "Probably reading books like the one you had for your compare-and-contrast paper." The pieces fell into place for Blake, and his face reddened with anger as his comprehension increased.

"Aunt Lisa, you said eavesdropping is not polite," Henriette complained.

"I apologize, Henriette. I was coming in to ask you to help me get supper started. Besides, I think Uncle Blake needs a drink of water."

"Are you okay, Uncle Blake? Your face is very red, and your hands are shaking."

"Deep breath, Blake. The internet has changed a lot of things, but in some ways, there's nothing new. It's just more accessible than it was back in our day." Aunt Lisa poured Blake a glass of water. "It's not that different from my parents' Italian student hosting a painting class at the Lutheran church. Remember, she complained everyone was so focused on the nude model that no one listened to her art lesson."

"We should talk to someone, at least to this Luke freak," Blake sputtered.

"No, we will not talk to Luke. We can teach Henriette what to say for herself and how to tell the difference between true and false friends. In my opinion, you are not helping her if you go bulldozing your way into her school and scare everyone away from her. Navigating social rules is always difficult. Now we have the added stress of learning both online and offline social rules."

"I need to go for a ride and scream into the wind," Blake muttered, straining to keep from swearing in front of Henriette again.

"I'm concerned for Uncle Blake," said Henriette. "Is he going to die?"

"No, he is not going to die. The motorcycle will be loud when he takes off, but you can trust me when I tell you that he's got his bike under control."

As the Harley revved, the kitchen window rattled, and Henriette slapped her hands over her ears. Aunt Lisa was prepared and pulled ear protectors from a drawer, gently holding them above Henriette's head.

"Do you want me to put these over your hands?" asked Lisa.

Henriette nodded. When she felt the earmuffs on her fingers, she moved her hands down and adjusted them.

"Better?" Aunt Lisa's muffled voice penetrated Henriette's anxiety fog.

Henriette nodded.

"I know this has been a stressful day so far, and we have all learned some new things. I think it is best if we turn the day around and get back to our schedule. I know the schedule says math, and that would not usually be a good idea. I can change today's lesson so it involves some M&Ms, which we can eat. We can do just a couple of steps or all of them. You let me know what you want to do when you are ready."

Aunt Lisa put an instruction sheet, candies, paper cups, markers, and paper on the table near Henriette. She knew Henriette would let her know when she was ready to start. Henriette seemed to ignore the materials for two minutes. Then she picked up the instruction sheet. As she read the items on the list, she moved them in front of her: a glass jar with a label that said "100 M&Ms," paper cups, and ten markers.

Henriette stopped working but didn't say anything. Aunt Lisa tapped the laminated white card on the table that stated "I need help."

Henriette picked up the card and handed it to her aunt. "I need help," Henriette said without looking at Lisa.

"You made a good start," Aunt Lisa answered encouragingly. "You followed the instructions to here. Is it okay if I cross off the steps that are already completed?"

Henriette nodded and saw Aunt Lisa cross out the line that said "Open the jar of 100 M&Ms." She saw step two, "Label each paper cup," remain.

"What does that mean?" asked Henriette.

"We need to sort the candies by color. On each paper cup, we will write a color. I have different colored pens so you can write the word *green* with the green pen, *red* with the red pen, and so on."

After Henriette finished labeling the ten paper cups, she began sorting the candies.

"I need help," Henriette said, looking up at Lisa.

"What do you need help with?" Aunt Lisa asked, smiling.

"I don't know what to do next," Henriette answered.

"Do you want me to tell you what do to, or do you want to guess by yourself first?"

"Is it okay if I guess wrong?" Henriette asked.

"Yes," answered Aunt Lisa. "Any guess is considered a good effort in my school."

"I think I need to count them."

"Correct," stated Aunt Lisa encouragingly. "Count and record. That means write down the color and put the number next to it."

When Henriette finished, she had a sheet of paper with the ten color names and the number ten written next to each.

"You have been doing great work, Henriette. I have one more new thing to tell you, and then you can be done for today. Is your brain ready for some new information?"

"A little."

"If I write a sentence about the candies, it takes a lot of time and space. For example, I'll write, 'Ten of the one hundred candies are red.' If I use math symbols to replace the words, it looks like this."

She pointed to wording that read, "10/100 red candies."

"Some people really like math because the math language of symbols makes more sense than words. Other people like words better because their brains find the symbols confusing. What do you prefer?"

"I like words better. Numbers and symbols are confusing."

"I understand. I need to do some writing now. What would you like to do for your break?"

"Can I watch TV?"

"Yes, you may. I think one of the game shows you like is on, but I'm not sure which channel."

"I know. I can find it." Henriette stood and walked a couple of steps. Impulsively, she came back and kissed Aunt Lisa's cheek. "Thank you, Aunt Lisa. You're a good math teacher."

CHAPTER TEN

The last night at the farm, Henriette couldn't fall asleep.

"Why does my stomach feel so icky?" Henriette asked Mully.

"Tomorrow is a change. Any change, even a good one, can give you butterflies in your stomach," answered Mully.

"Eww, that's gross. Why do humans talk like that? Say stuff that isn't real just to be weird."

"I can't explain all the things humans say," Mully said. "But I do know the fluttering in your stomach and shakiness is anxiety about change. Calm breathing and some logical questions are a good place to start if you want to decrease your anxiety and increase your confidence in your problem-solving ability."

"I am a good problem solver when you help me. Can you come with me back to my home?"

"That's not for me to say. You would have to ask Lisa and Blake."

"I could put you in my suitcase. No one would notice."

"Taking things without asking is stealing, even when no one notices. It would be better for you to ask your aunt for permission to let me stay with you for a while. Also, if you really need help, just stop and think, *What would Mully say?*"

"Would you like to come stay with me for a while?"

"A visit would be nice, but I would want to come back to my farm eventually."

In the morning, Henriette went down to breakfast, holding Mully.

Aunt Lisa glanced at her and then put a pancake on a plate and placed it in front of her. "I was thinking. You have only been here for two weeks, and I don't want you to forget all the good things we've worked on. Is there something you would like to take back home with you to help you remember us?"

"I'd like to take Mully home with me for a visit. When he's homesick, I will bring him back to the farm."

"Is that Mully?" asked Aunt Lisa.

"Yes," answered Henriette.

"Blake, do you remember the harlequin your grandparents used to argue about every Christmas?" Lisa motioned for Blake to join them at the kitchen table.

"The one with the artsy face? Grandpa said he was hideous, but Grandma called him so ugly that he was cute."

"Yes, well, Henriette has discovered his name is Mully. You did say him, didn't you? Him, not her?"

"Yes, this time he's a him. Sometimes he's a her, but this time, he's a him," said Henriette matter-of-factly.

"That makes sense to me. Would you like to take Mully with you back to the city?" Blake asked.

"Yes, if that's okay with you," Henriette said.

"You bet," said Uncle Blake.

Henriette smiled and gave Uncle Blake a high five. "You bet!"

Mary Ayetey (right) and Rachel McDonald (left) pictured at Maplewood Area Historical Society's Bruentrup Heritage Farm, Maplewood, MN

ABOUT THE AUTHORS

Mary Ayetey and Rachel McDonald live in a small house on a busy street of Maplewood, Minnesota. Maplewood is a suburb of St. Paul, the capital of Minnesota, and much of the land now filled with homes was farmland just fifty years ago.

Rachel McDonald and Mary Ayetey are a mother and daughter who have both enjoyed writing and other creative projects on their own. In coming together to write a fictional novel based on some personal experiences, many convoluted bits of information collected from public schools, social media, and the area of Minnesota familiar to them, they found themselves creating a new voice as they wrote together. Thus, it seemed only natural to combine their names. Most people have difficulty guessing at the pronunciation of Mary's last name. Her father recommended using the number eighty (80) for simplification, but, alas, it became one too many things to explain, so their first names were combined and May Rae was brought into existence.

Rachel McDonald, as mother, long-time caregiver, and graduate of many college degree programs (AAS, BA, and MA), knew, in order to maintain the core language and behavior of the central characters, the story would have to be self-published. The project remained frozen in an unfinished state due to the conundrum of staying true to the heart of the ASD storyteller while responding to friends' informal editing and questions.

The project would have remained stalled—like an April cold front stalled over Minnesota — if not for the unknowing, unsolicited advice of Rachel's older brother, Philip, who is also Mary's godfather. "We can all strive to do something extraordinary, and in the meantime, we can all enjoy the extraordinary beauty of the ordinary." He had not been informed that the cursed virus known as "writer's block" had infested our story. He simply was sharing a thought about words, like ordinary and extraordinary. That, in a nutshell, was the problem.

Autism, Bruentrup Farm, a funny-looking doll that came from some great-grandparents' farmhouse attic, and imaginary voices offering advice and support, these are all ordinary things in our life. Mary tries to express what she is thinking, dealing with neurotypicals constantly saying, "Your words aren't making sense. Can you say it another way?" They are oblivious to the immense effort it took for her to speak.

And Rachel is filling in the gaps from their shared experiences, translating between the ASD brains and the neurotypical brains. Together, their indomitable spirits find ways to make all this work of navigating everyday life fun and humorous through songs, stories, puppets, and craft projects. This is all very ordinary for us.

ENDNOTES

1 Facebook post of Philip Hughes-Luing on March 11—My epiphany for the day inspired by the Oregon Humanities Death and Dying conversation this afternoon hosted by the Grants Pass Museum of Art

www.ingramcontent.com/pod-product-compliance
Lightning Source LLC
Chambersburg PA
CBHW041522120626
46551CB00018B/2536